At The River's Edge
Where Quantum Streams Flow

Yvonne L. Jones

DEDICATION

For all those awakening to that inner voice.
This book is dedicated to you.

CONTENTS

ACKNOWLEDGMENTS

How does one begin to acknowledge all the inspiring
balladeers and unsung heroes for their part in helping
to shape, encourage and pull or push a body along?
The acknowledgement page would be longer than the
entire book if I made the attempt. ☺
Therefore, I will acknowledge this--that I could not
have done it alone.
Thank you!

1

THINKING LIKE WATER

I cleansed my cup
Made ready a vessel one could not corrupt
Prepared my throat for a long, satisfying sip
Went to the well, drawing deep, needing more than a dip
Intending to fill my cup well past overflowing
Be impregnated like a sponge
With waters of universal knowing.

I was ready, open for the waters that quench
Expecting to be completely and irreversibly drenched
So fathom my surprise at the well being dry
Of my concern what such emptiness might possibly imply
That my well had been tapped, diminished by another
Or by my own neglect, it would sustain no other.

As my hopes seemed destined to the altar for slaughter
I smiled, how foolish of me for not thinking like water
With renewed abandon and joy I dove into the well

Yvonne L. Jones

To be carried away by still waters that swelled
The immersion revived hopes and dreams downtrodden
And whispered of things I should never have forgotten.

"I will feed, cleanse and carry you when you falter or tire
Push, pull and lift you as high as you aspire
Drought and barrenness have no hold on me
For I am inexhaustible and exist in unlimited forms
It is impossible to drink too much
To deplete or do me any harm.

Cease any struggles to control, change or hinder
Those things not within your power
For living waters that flow eternal
Will cover you every second, minute and hour.

Know that you are fluid, spirit
A powerful droplet infused with liquid fire
Alone or in numbers
A force to be reckoned, a peace to be desired.

That I am your contagion and remedy
Your fulfillment and release
The beloved and lover, your curtailment and increase
Remember who you are great sons and great daughters
True reflections of The Source
When you are thinking like water."

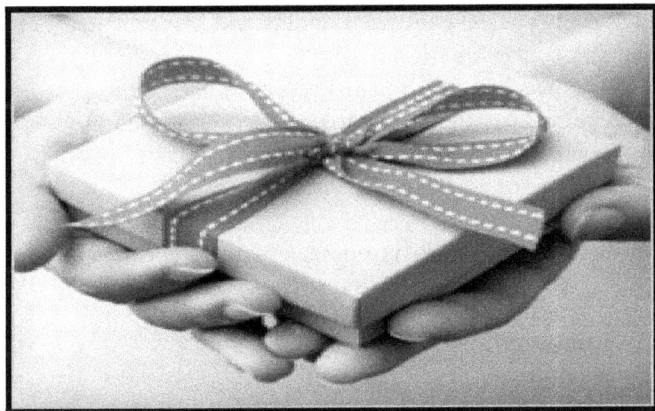

2
THE GIFT

We each have been recipients of many gifts
Some were simple and easy to come by
While others seemed difficult to understand
Or to appreciate and enjoy
Yet all of them have been worth unwrapping.

For how do we not in some way
Love and honor each mirror-soul we encounter
Each moment we are given?
As there is no one soul or one moment
Greater than that which exist within this present gift.

We and the present are one
And even when we fall back to the past
Or leap forward into the future
It's accomplished while remaining exactly where we are
In this present moment
So as you uncover your many gifts

Deeply consider and then understand why you are.
That you are as strong
Or as weak as the thoughts you hold onto
As brave or as timid as the dreams you subdue
As blessed or as cursed as the words you speak
As sharp or as dull as the vision you seek.

That you are uplifted or defiled by the choices you make
Happy or miserable by the actions you take
And whether you flow like water
Or become rigid like stone
This never-ending gifting cycle
Of present, of moment, of now
Is never wrong.

You will always be why you are
And it doesn't matter if you feel great or small
Or in between
You are as magical dust exploding from heavenly stars
Loving, experiencing, witnessing all that there is
And forever awakening to the new
Now is the moment you should stop wondering
"Is there another why?"
No, there is only the gift of you.

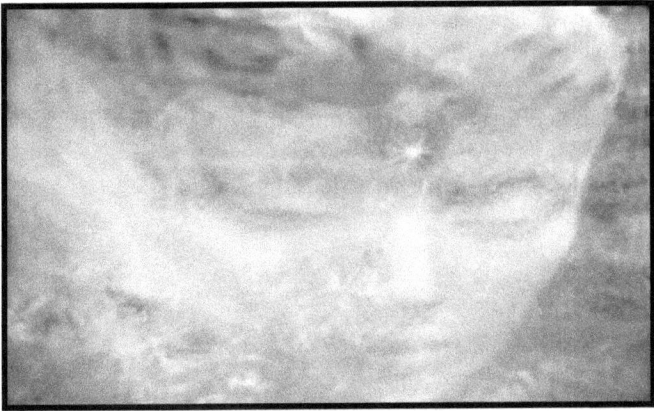

3

MYSTERIOUS MYSTERY

There is a mystery the mind seeks to unfold
A mist of knowledge that beckons one and all to behold
An overflow of substance rejuvenating body and soul
It leaves a trail, subtle hints
Hidden clues within feelings, sounds and scents
But tarry and the lead grows cold.

Why do you wait
Where is wisdom as you stand just outside of sate
Does your empty cup not tempt you to propagate
Or does carrying nothing better suit your taste?

Woe to the one who will not seek
This mystery the mysterious sanctions you greet
Blessed are those ignoring the call to retreat
Yet advancing towards the One
The soul insist they must meet.

Why woe if you say no and blessed if you say yes
Is it easier to drink from an empty cup
Do you desire more rather than less
Can you imagine sharing one which is overflowing
Is that not by far the best
Shall a simple yea or nay determine the rest?

If you refuse to see
How can you show
If you hold the seed
When does another grow
If you ignore the call
Can anyone hear what you know
If upon your shaky ground you intend to stand
How many will stumble and fall below?

When you seek not the mystery
You hinder more than self
For no soul is an island or an empty shelf
You were created to hold for eternity
Things of wonder, things that help
And not to begrudge the existence you were dealt.

It awaits you, therefore it is attainable
Is everlasting and fully sustainable
Seeks you just as you seek it
Nourishes and protects you if you will permit

The mystery is really no mystery at all
Though it loves to mesmerize and enthrall
It waits patiently beneath a covering in plain view
If you would but look you'd know that you already knew
The mysterious mystery awaiting
Is you!

4

CAULDRON OF SOULS

My soul is a cauldron, a tempest
Churning, revolving, imploding, exploding
An endless vessel of release
Of emptying out and filling once again
It is light and night, dark and day
A black hole of emptiness encased in infinite luminosity

It delights in taking flight beyond this universe
As it sits immobile behind two small sees
When all else sleeps, it awakens and dreams of creation
By multiplying seven times seven
And rounding off at one.

My soul is a cauldron, shaped in inequity
Fashioned from pure thought
Energized by vibrational cosmic matter
It is never ending, all knowing
Hind and foresight, voice and silence

The bottom that always drops
A ceiling that never stops
Contained yet unchained
An untapped abundance leaving nothing behind.

Oh, how I love my soul
A cauldron of universal proportions
It is star dust, star light, galaxies and planets
Every being, all matter
A gentle nothingness with form and substance
That blindly reflects all.

It is a question for the answer
An error-less mishap
The center of left behind right
A blood thirsty lover and a conqueror of peace
The sensitive Joker and the warrior Priest
It is for one as it is for all
My soul is a soul of the Soul experiencing souls.

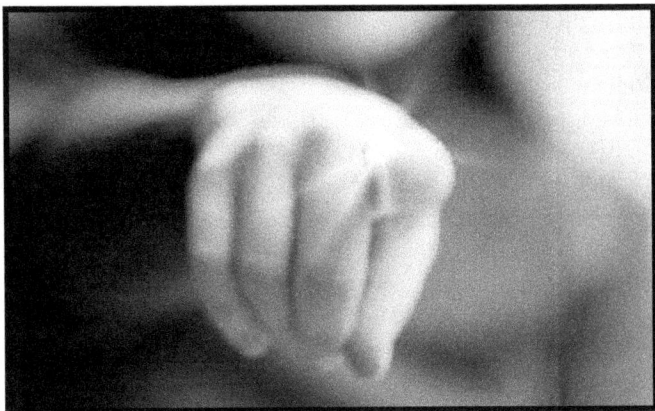

5

HEY YOU THERE!

Hey, you there!

Dancing along the limitless pathways of my being
Moving in graceful rhythm, perfecting soulful choreography
With each step, step, sway, you move me through space
Rewriting my self-proclaimed history
Liberating and exhilarating, dancing with you is so freeing
Move me with your soul so I can never leave you.

Hey, you there!

The light that transforms deepest darkness to bright
Yet your glow does not singe me or corrupt my sight
Drawn I am like a moth to a flame
Consumed yet instantly born again
Shine on me to chase the cold away
Bathe me in your iridescence
That I might know your radiant array.

Yvonne L. Jones

Hey, you there!

So light-hearted and full of glee
Tickling my funny bone with a riddle
A conundrum or a paradigm
Delighting in the puzzlement I sometimes convey
Yet overjoyed when I eventually find my way.

A challenger who's sure and steady
Self-commanding, bold and war ready
The Knight who skillfully trumps the King
But gentle when engaging or entertaining the Queen.

Hey, you there!

The accomplished mathematician's son
Who knew without boasting
That one plus one always equals one
Accomplished at rendering thoughts like a poet laureate
The stuff of life, those moving symbols I cannot forget.

Reciting vibrational verse from this ever unfolding Universe
Drawing from memory with artistic flair, unrehearsed
Inspired echoes now etched upon the canvas of my mind
That willing medium your creativity endeavors to entwine.

Hey, you there!

6
ENGIMA UNLEASHED

There once was a time when I only knew
The things my senses led me to
But since that time I've moved beyond
All the facts and stats others have spawned
I've moved inside and there I reside
Where inner truth and outer confusion coincide.
I now anxiously wait
Aggressively watch and agilely listen
As I am moved to stay still
To take flight
To be present
To disappear
To transition.

I find eternity in the place where I exist no more
I'm as infinite and simple as the element zero
Sheer as sun light, none can pass through me
So densely packed, I rise like a wish on a plea.

Yvonne L. Jones

I'm seeable if you cease to look
Easily found abandoned within a hidden nook
You may forget with me the sound noise employs
Then remember the sweetness of silence's roar
It's my melody of choice
The pureness of quiet thoughts lifts this spirit's voice.

I'll beseech you to exercise stillness and actively rest
Help you tally every star in the cosmos
Every grain of sand North, South, East and West
I will only hold you if you are freedom's bond
Release you as you slave to behave
Nourish you when you become too full of yourself
Be the memory of things you attempt to forget.

I will love you when you love me not
See your path as you wonder about
Hear when your lips confirm or deny
Sense the hand you play as you hide and conspire
I will never judge your questions, answers or silence
Nor condemn you for willful neglect and misguidance.

For there once was a time when I only knew
The things my senses led me to
But since that time I've moved beyond
All the facts and stats others have spawned
I've moved inside and there I reside
Where inner truth and outer confusion coincide.
I now anxiously wait
Aggressively watch and agilely listen
As I am moved to stay still
To take flight
To be present
To disappear
To transition.

7
THE HIDDEN

Helpful gestures, an attentive ear, sincerity of the eye
A voice smooth and shiny, slippery as silk
Perfect manners sparkling against an ominous sky
Masterful creator of pleasures that grow and flow
Beneath echoes of soothing melodies
Such saintly tasks and reported good deeds
Solicit rewarding remedies
What better way to camouflage and fool
Hidden truths simmering just beneath the cool.

Indecent power moves, brutal confrontations
Approves of little to nothing
Delights in boisterous altercations
A cantankerous sullen one
Hopelessly lost in abstract facts
A raging tempest firing off insults
The boiler at its max
Such gruff exchanges makes it easier to unseat

Yvonne L. Jones

Hidden truths chilling just beneath the heat.

Depression, full of sadness
Thoughts the color of deepest blue
Ashes piled upon the head
Covers a life deemed unworthy of review
A hoped-for madness to replace a self-induced debility
Downcast to pensive
Sober to the point of invisibility
Feeling lower than low should serve to end it all
Hidden truths elevating just before the fall.

Dapper to the ninth degree
Classic or trendy in due season
Free to indulge in flamboyant exhibitions
Often for no good reason
Ignoring any plea to refrain from pomp
Regardless of circumstance
Unwilling to not out-shine another
Or to risk the loss of a fleeting, second glance
An idol power infused within a dress to impress
To cover that which is truly lacking
Hidden truths unraveling
Bursting just beneath the tacking.

Each one carries a penchant for The Hidden
Be it for gain or at cost
Rather for need or what's strictly forbidden
Some harbor a few, others carry far too many
Whatever the number
The Hidden outweighs the plenty

There lurking within and pushing its way out
Are the untold spores of fear and uncertainty
Pollenating, contaminating man's glorious destiny
But if reason would shine its all seeing light

At The River's Edge Where Quantum Streams Flow

On shades of needs, wants and atrocities
Hidden truths will be hidden no more
But unveiled, revealing all disguises.

Yvonne L. Jones

8
HOW LONG?

How long
Will you ignore the truth and believe the lie
Ransom your mind, body and soul
For a two-minute high?

How long
Will you rise every morning
Reeking of fear, ignorance and self-hate
Then boast of a race you clearly cannot appreciate?

How long
Will you exhaust your energy
Engage in trivial pursuits
Remain unaware, unconcerned, unmoved
By the gene pool you dilute?
Strife, Misery, Complacency
All relevant names for your offspring
A dying tree sprouting sick roots

Too diseased to heal the fruit it strings.

How long
Will you point your crooked finger
Split your forked tongue
Assume the world will think you've changed
Chanting the same old song?
Eager to shove mock philosophy
Down the throats of the meek and true
Then disrupt the tide
When the natural flow threatens to overtake you.

How long
Will you strut like a peacock
Slither like a snake
Chest-pound like a primate
Arrogantly displaying untold mistakes?
Proud in dishonor, steadfast in contempt
Blind as a bat, foolishly believing you're morally exempt.

How long
Will you continue to exist outside of the dream
Living in a nightmare
Chasing shadows, perpetrating a scheme?
Never seeing your end or believing it will ever come
But the beat is winding down
Deliverance quiets the drum.

9

SONG OF THE FOREST

Before time, human thought and language could spew
I was here waiting patiently for you
Before you ever wondered or formed questions about me
I had already given the answers, planted the seed
Pruned the tree.

Before huts, cultivated fields and roads of stone
I was here guiding and prompting you on
Before man-made structures and inspired works of art
I gave of myself
Yours were the creations from my thoughts
Before you learned how to heal or chose when to kill
I covered and protected you, the exalted ones of my will.

How quickly have you forgotten how to seek me out in awe
To know the way, to reach for light
To never cower, to stand ready for flight
Instead, you remember me not

Yvonne L. Jones

Yet communes with that which chains you to a law
Trading your priceless freedom for trinkets
For things of lesser substance than dry ink.

Why cover yourself in worthless adornments
Presenting what was once great as lesser fragments
Do you not remember before the mass slumber
That you were perfect, already complete?

Now you're lost, unawake, depleted
Stumbling about in your own path
Existing without knowing your fate
Believing you're walking straight
You accept great loss with the choice of never seeing
When all is yours simply for being.

Do you believe the forest is but trees
That all rains, rivers and oceans end at seas
Or that lots, those divided plots of your world
Is but dead dirt carved from an unconscious planet
Or that the heaven's is only a picture window
Designed to showcase exploding gases and floating granite?

Can you create a leaf, a twig, a pebble or dirt
Without one single element from beneath my skirt
Will you soar without the wind around you
Land without wings to safely ground you
Do you see with your feet, hear with your fingers
Focus your eyes to enjoy a scent that pleasantly lingers?

Yet you trod upon those outside of your view
Accuse others who choose to sit and wonder at my pew
Bind the eyes, hands and voices of those made aware
Of your cataracts, clinched fist and forked tongue
Those deadly snares.

At The River's Edge Where Quantum Streams Flow

Know this, there is a season for all
That the higher leaf will one day wither and fall
And at its decent, it will surely cry out in dismay
But it is the leaf responsible for its demise in this way
Did you not witness through this cycle of living
That one eventually receives what one is giving?

Come back to your roots
For mine knows no bottom
Stay connected to the vine
Bypass the harshness of autumn
Renew your seeking
For my branch's reach is unlimited
I am the One, the first and the last forest
All things come and go within it.

Gather from the great forest floor, twigs
Weave your nests securely within my branches
Or position them between trunk and root
And be covered by a living canopy that enhances.

Eat of my fruit, sip dew from my leaves
Be nourished, sustained and healed of what grieves you
So when much of you has grown enough
There will be no more mistaking
You have always and forever will be
A great and mighty forest in the making.

Yvonne L. Jones

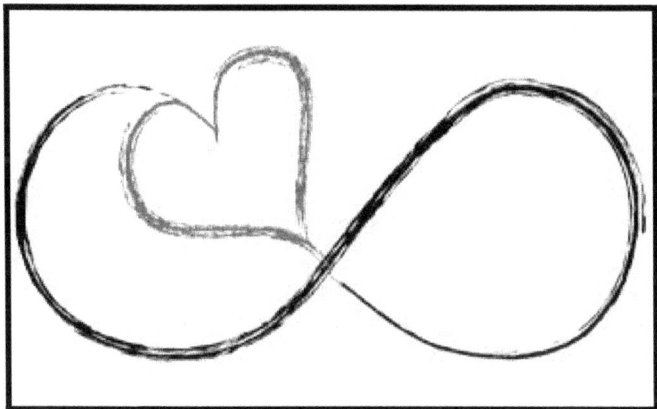

10
LOVE'S ANSWER

Is it even possible to lose one's self in love
Or do we merely dive deep
Beneath the bottomless swell of love's pull
Connecting to that which was once hidden
If I am love do I need more of it
Or a different version of love's expression from another?

If love be complete
Why does it feel the need to grow
Will we find secured within love's completeness
The ability to self-duplicate
To swallow up the sands of time
Or to reach beyond a never-ending Universe
While surpassing depths unknown
Is this the magic love performs with such perfection
That it simply is, therefore I Am?

Should I dare to wonder at love's point of origin

Yvonne L. Jones

If it began inside the steady organ of one with rhythm
Or that it will someday cease to be
When the rhythmic beating returns to clay
And yet if love is never for not
Nor is it ever out of season
How then can it be found nestled within one's fragile heart
If love is the heart of all existence?

Haven't we spent more time then need be
Ignoring the beauty of love's majestic displays
Walked away, ran from, feared the outcome of
The most important means of abundance in life
Why do we hate what heals us
Or find it easier to abandon
The only structure that fortifies
Why do we starve ourselves to death
When sustenance is so close at hand?

If you will open your mind to converse with love, do listen
As the scales fall away and your vision clears, please see it
Only then, after your heart has bled out
And there's nothing left to hinder you
Let love fill it
So you can feel again and understand your purpose
For yours is not occupation, talent, beauty or wit
It is and always will be
The art of loving well.

11
WISHING YOU

At the dawn of a never ending sunrise
When wakefulness comes as a pleasant surprise
As that ebbing light glides across twilight skies
And you empty your vessel
Of concerns that compromise
I'm wishing you happy, smiling
And looking deeply into my eyes.

Laughter while dark clouds gather
Hope when disaster seems to tether
Strength as opposition joins together
Flexibility to never break but to float like a feather
I'm wishing you resilience to bear any weather.

Clarity to assist in that which needs gauging
Tolerance that increases in awareness and stages
Wisdom that embraces those of the ages
A testament to the Enlightened Ones, the Sage's

Yvonne L. Jones

I'm wishing you the Book of Life
Of never ending pages.

Days of joy, hours of bliss
Moments of quiet contemplation
Coupled with mere seconds
That ignite soulful revelations.

New and broad horizons yet explored
Deep and vast oceans of anticipation
A journey that never ends
An existence full of aspirations
I'm wishing you my love
Nothing short of inspired creation.

I'm wishing you.

12
YINGING AND YANGING

I form a thought
You deliver the perfect rendition
I relive a battle badly fought
You reign victorious in every mission.

I hear a haunting melody
You finely tune each note
Should I feel the weight of life's intensity
You lift us above it, we literally float.

If I am at a loss and scattered
Like a laser, you remain on point
When I expose a vessel devoid of matter
You fill it past the rim
Overflowing my cup as you anoint.

I seek a hidden treasure
You stand before me

Shimmering like a jewel in the night
I ransom pleasure
You deliver unimaginable desires and delights.

In my awkward attempts to express
You simply utter the unspoken
When I forget never to regret
You remind me that I'm not broken.

If I fail to understand my own needs
You know them as a lesson taught
As I struggle to arrive, to succeed
You nudge or carry me till I want for naught.

I, you, we, be
Where one begins, the other ends
You, I, be, we
Yinging and Yanging as we ascend.

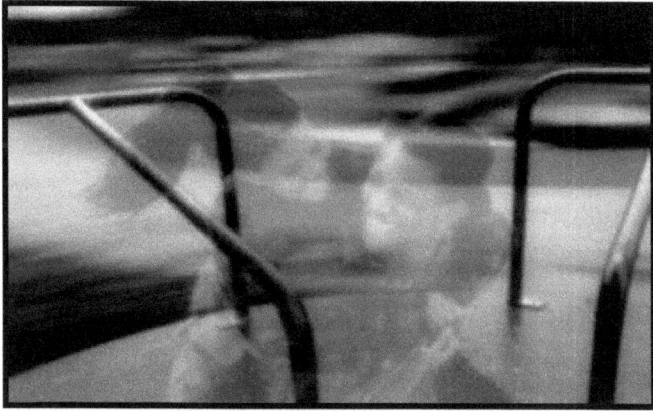

13
SMILE'S PLAY

As I lay awake in the wee hours of the night
I feel your smile playing as if at recess
In the amusement park of my mind.
It tumbles and somersaults, slides across my face
Just like a ball player rushing in from third base.

Oh, how it leans back in the swings
Soaring higher with each attempt
To touch my mind, my sky, my temple, my eye.
Just one final push back and over the top it goes
It amazes me how happy it seems to be
As it entertains itself while pleasing me.

Jumping off the swings
And hopping on the merry-go-round
Your smile pulls me along
Prompting me to let go, to throw up my arms.
I'm still dizzy from all the spinning

The whirling, the twirling
But then it's off to the next ride
Where more fun awaits
And not for one moment
Does your smile pause or hesitate.

I feel your smile as it dances through my heart
Sense its urging as it slumbers when we're apart
See it as it lands and lights, dances and takes flight
Know that it was always meant to play
In my park, on my grounds and throughout my days.

I will always cherish your smile's play.

14

THE MAKING OF YOU

A galaxy within a galaxy where time no longer exist
Like a full moon nestled in a blazing hot sun
Straddling stars, jetting across an endless ink-black sky
You rise, you ebb and flow, you burn, you glow
A Super Nova expanding beyond the Universe
I see the making of you.

Like thick green grass
Springing back with each step that I take
Or grains of white, glistening sand
Igniting my soles, my fingers, my hands
With a whirlwind of colors, you cover each morn
Crystal blue, golden yellow and tempting orange

Then at dusk, you reclaim the brush
Painting my nights, saturating my head
With blushing pinks, royal purples and burning reds
An ever evolving will of pure artistry

Yvonne L. Jones

I can feel the making of you.

Did you not know
That a glimpse of you would change my bearing
My understanding, my me
Or did you sense without knowing
Your mystical persuasions could also set me free
Does a wonder even know what a wonder it truly is?

I cannot help but imprint you, place you in my DNA
Dive into, float above, sink beneath, stowaway
Because you have poured yourself out
Allowing me to flow within
It is there where I intend to reside
Inside the making of you.

15
IF I COULD SEE YOU NOW

If I could see you now
What would your eyes reveal
Will I catch my reflection in them
See the joy my presence gives
Witness depths of wonder behind each open lid
Or know that understanding is alive inside?

If I could see you now
What would your lips reveal
Happiness in the corners of every smile
A child-like playfulness, merriment and delight
The absence of judgement or anger and contempt
Or that they're lightly pressed together
In contemplation of a desired task?

If I could see you now
What would your heart reveal
How it beats for more than one
That it embodies the secrets of eternal love

Is as open as an unbound book
Or moves with compassion where others forsook?

If I could see you now
What would your hands reveal
Their power within a tender caress
Restraint from confinement or causing any harm
How they join together in supplication and thanksgiving
Or so easily embraces the hands of a beloved?

If I could see you now
What would your back reveal
Strength and suppleness depicting a character unbroken
That between its span are arms of bounty and of might
How it lays down, holds up
Or arches at a touch without a fight
And would never turn towards me in displeasure
Nor contempt?

If I could see you now
What would your loins reveal
How you are certain of who you are
That I more than please you
And that you will rise to conquer the urge
Or be content to merely hold me in peace?

If I could see you now
What would your feet reveal
Their ability to lead us in the right direction
To never tire in the walk or journey mapped together
The ability and willingness to stand or to backup
Steadfastness when going around a stumbling block
Or confidence in seeking higher ground
When turbulent waters seek us out
If I could see you now
I'd know of the wonders you'd reveal.

Yvonne L. Jones

ABOUT THE AUTHOR

Yvonne L. Jones is a native of Houston, Texas. She is an Inspirational Life Coach in training and the author of another book of poetry, *"Speaking Out and Listening In."*

For information about the author, new books and audio release dates or the benefits of becoming a VIP reader, visit:

littlesepiabooks.com

If you have enjoyed this Little Sepia Book, please take just a moment and give it an honest review at:

amazon.com/author/yvonne

Thank You!